The Business In You

Unleashing the Entrepreneur

By

Eugene L. Moore, MBA, Ph.D.

LIFE TO LEGACY

The Business In You:

Unleashing the Entrepreneur

By Eugene L. Moore, Copyright 2019

ISBN: 978-1-947288-53-9

10 9 8 7 6 5 4 3 2 1

Printed in the United States of America

Cover design by: Treviante Brown
Back cover photo by: Steven Williams III

Published by: Life To Legacy, LLC
P.O. Box 1239
Matteson, IL 60443
877-267-7477
www.Life2Legacy.com

Contents

About the Author   5

Acknowledgments   8

Foreword I   10

Foreword II   12

Preface   14

Introduction   15

1. See It   18

2. Seize It   22

3. Scrutinize It   28

4. Simplify It   33

5. Sell It   37

6. Sustain It   41

7. Support It   45

Conclusion   49

Presented To

SEND EMAILS TO:
info@assurancecreekyouth.org

About the Author

IT HAS BEEN JUST OVER A YEAR SINCE EUGENE L. MOORE, MBA, Ph.D. published his fifth book titled *Mentors Matter but Poverty Sucks,* which focuses on the vileness of poverty and the effects it has on some of the most vulnerable populations within one of the richest nations in the world. Hopefully, after reading the book, readers learned the systemic nature of poverty and the explosive power education could have to curtail some of its inherent causalities.

As Eugene neared the completion of his MBA from the Gies College of Business at the University of Illinois at Urbana-Champaign, his fervor to speak to marginalized voices intensified and he felt inclined to publish a book that focuses on the business acumen he believes all people innately possess. Thus, he put pen to paper to write a book which anyone could read and learn basic tenants of business without overuse of convoluted rhetoric which deters some from exploring their business interests.

His latest book titled *The Business in You: Unleashing the Entrepreneur* is yet another example of his efforts to pay it forward. He pulls from his international travel, consulting partnerships, corporate experience, and his education to deliver a must read to those who want to start their own business. It is not intended for those who desire instant fame and fortune, but those who aspire to move their thoughts to tangible actions. Business is about results, not mere hyperbole which at best might garner interest, but lacks substance and sustainability. One of the first questions any aspiring entrepreneur should ask themselves is, what product or service am I providing and what need does it satisfy? Your desire to become a business owner should never be solely birthed out of your desire to escape the pressures and demands of corporate America, higher education, government, or the non-profit sector, but because you unequivocally satisfy a need in which customers are willing to pay.

Eugene wrote the book specifically to demystify the misconceptions surrounding entrepreneurship. In fact, he clearly articulates how business ownership is not easy and in most cases is more difficult than any C-Suite position one might hold. Entrepreneurship requires tenacity and resilience that even some of the most zealous executives do not necessarily have in their repertoire. *The Business in You: Unleashing the Entrepreneur* will leave readers with a clearer picture of what it means to be an entrepreneur which is initially a person or persons who serve as a generalist for some time until the business reaches maturity. If your business, despite how noble or socially conscious, fails to secure meaningful profits, then it will be forced to dissolve despite the passion, intellect, or business prowess of the owner(s).

Although some nonprofit organizations operate with a budget deficit, even they are not exempt from the consequences of having more expenses than revenue. Hence, understanding "the why" of your business endeavor is critical to your success, coupled with how the work will be accomplished because failure to do so will have grave consequences.

In addition to working for the University of Illinois, he serves as the President and Chief Executive Officer of Assurance Creek Youth Program, Inc. and as a consultant to various global business enterprises. His latest book serves as an example of his commitment to using his gifts, talents, and resources to help others. Dr. Eugene L. Moore firmly believes education is power and if you desire for that power to have a compounded effect, you must share it with as many people as possible.

Acknowledgments

I RECALL WHEN I FIRST BEGAN MY BUSINESS VENTURE AND LIKE most children the lemonade stand seemed to be one of the most feasible options for an eight-year-old kid. My overhead cost was zero as my mother paid for all the supplies, making my profit somewhat inflated. After having a successful lemonade stand, I created a greeting card business which also rendered great profits, but my first failure came when I wrote my first book titled, *The 21st Century, What Will It Be Like,* at thirteen years old.

Although, my neighbors, family members, and friends were willing to pay for the book, it was never published. Despite this unforeseen heartbreak, my love for business intensified when I became a member of Junior Achievement in elementary school. However, my second failure came during my first year in college when I learned I would not be accepted into the College of Business. I was determined not to give up on my dream and decided to major in communication because I felt having effective communication skills seemed appropriate for an aspiring business professional.

When I graduated from undergrad, my appetite for business had not subsided, and after a brief stint in the corporate sector, I returned to school to pursue a Master of Education in Human Resources. Similar to communication, I felt having a grasp on how to manage human capital was an invaluable resource for a business leader. With great enthusiasm, I accepted a job offer with a Fortune 5 company. The experience was simply amazing, but I returned to school to receive my doctorate as my social consciousness had risen to a level that required immediate action. Then my life came full circle as I decided to pursue my MBA and now I realize what deserves the greatest acknowledgment for this book and my entire life.

I am deeply grateful for my failures, denial letters, and multiple rejections because it provided the greatest lesson I have ever learned, which is to never surrender your passion, and for that, I say thank you.

Foreword I

ENTREPRENEURSHIP MAY BE CONSIDERED ONE OF THE MOST important pillars of our society. The question of whether or not entrepreneurs are "born" or "made" is frequently asked. In *The Business in You: Unleashing the Entrepreneur,* Dr. Eugene Moore provides practical insights and strategies that anyone can use in developing an entrepreneurial mindset. This book not only distills important concepts, but it encourages the reader to pursue their business ideas but in a measured and thoughtful way.

In this book, Dr. Moore builds upon the premise that everyone has unique gifts and talents that may provide the opportunity to build a business that creates value for others. I believe that this is true. *The Business in You: Unleashing the Entrepreneur* demystifies entrepreneurship through its use of examples of entrepreneurs and some of the challenges that they experienced. Dr. Moore focuses on seven essential steps to unleashing the entrepreneur in you – *See it, Seize it, Scrutinize it, Simplify it, Sell it, Sustain it,* and *Support it.* These seven steps are independent of the type of business that you may choose to start. These steps provide a useful process for framing your thinking.

As I think back to four years ago when we started the social for-profit venture, Sun Buckets, Inc., the concepts and the 7 steps articulated by Dr. Moore resonates loudly. Step 1 is to focus on the vision and mission. The mission of Sun Buckets is to address the global cooking crisis where nearly three billion people live with inadequate access to energy for cooking. Additionally, indoor air pollution from cooking results in nearly 3 million deaths annually. Step 2 is to focus on pursuing the opportunity. We had the novel idea of addressing this challenge using thermal energy storage, which is uniquely different from current solar cookers on the market. In Step 3, scrutinizing the business idea, we focused very intentionally on consumer/end-user behavior. What were the pain points when cooking in these areas with limited energy access? What are the limitations to current solar cookers and their adoption? As we move forward to Step 4, making the case for the existence of our business, we continued to circle back to the question of why is thermal energy storage the best alternative? As we moved to step 5, *Sell it*, we became very aware of the need to build relationships with the stakeholders – NGOs, ministries of energy, financial partners, local communities, and supply chain partners. In seeking strategies for sustaining Sun Buckets, we focused on a business model that places an emphasis on strengthening the economies of the local communities in which Sun Buckets products are deployed. Finally, one of the most important needs is building a team to support the growth. We have 15 team members that are dedicated to helping Sun Buckets make a lasting impact.

The importance of entrepreneurship and entrepreneurs in our society cannot be overstated. This insightful book by Dr. Eugene Moore provides critical techniques that we can apply to unleash the business in us.

—Joe Bradley
Sun Buckets, Inc.

Foreword II

SOMETIMES THE ANSWER TO THE QUESTION IS STARING you right in the face. Would-be entrepreneurs often ask themselves, "What kind of business should I start?" Well, what are you interested in? Many successful entrepreneurs began their research with the familiar; did pertinent research to assess viability; then moved onto other ideas. The key point is that nothing happens without first taking a step. Entrepreneurs should not only explore the familiar but also consult with knowledgeable experts in their circles. Everyone won't have access to a consulting firm but if you have an aunt who's an accountant or an uncle who's a salesperson, then you have resources in your circle to not only help you unleash the entrepreneur within you but also develop key business skills.

Mindset is also a key component to unleashing the entrepreneur in you. Who do you associate with? What do you read? It's one thing to light the fire but good entrepreneurs are able to sustain it until it is ready to burn on its own. When people study the titans of business like Buffett, Gates and Zuckerberg, the commonality they find is that they are voracious readers, constant seekers of knowledge.

What's your motivation? Do you enjoy what you do on a daily basis? If not, are you prepared to pay the price? You can only answer these questions by searching out the entrepreneur in you. This book is a great tool to help you begin that journey. It will provide some answers. In some cases, it will generate new questions for you to seek out the answers. One thing is certain though if you are interested in unleashing the entrepreneur in you, reading this book is a great start!

—Erick Harris
Regional Sales Manager

Preface

BUSINESS HAS AN INHERENT MESSINESS TO IT AND FOR some it is off-putting but for others, it is the driving force behind their desire to become the next great business leader. However, one of the biggest misconceptions is that every great idea can become a great business. On the contrary, many great ideas do not translate into a successful business. Many hopeful entrepreneurs fail to even start their business because they have focused on commonly known statistics which state that their chances of failure are almost inevitable especially over a five-year period.

This book aims to provide a more optimistic view about starting a business and it is not necessarily so you can quit your day job. *The Business in You: Unleashing the Entrepreneur* hopes to provide readers with useful and practical strategies to form a business. Perhaps you enjoy baking and have been inundated by family and friends to make your delicious pound cake and apple pie. The question is, does this heightened demand suggest you should invest your entire life's savings to start your own bakery company? It depends. In fact, after reading this book you will have a definitive answer and for some, the orders from family and friends will be the depth of your business venture and for others, it will constitute a successful bakery business that defies the odds of a small startup.

Do note this book is not designed to unmask the secrets of conglomerate companies like 21st Century Fox or Walt Disney, nor highly successful companies like Google, Facebook or Apple, but you will see some similarities as no successful business, big or small succeeds without great products and services.

Introduction

Prospective and current entrepreneurs are always seeking knowledge whether it comes from Forbes, Bloomberg, the Wall Street Journal, the Economist, NPR, or Google. Others are inclined to seek advice from successful business leaders and knowledge contributors like Napoleon Hill, Steve Jobs, Peter Drucker, Jeff Bezos, Tim King, Warren Buffett, Bill Gates, Mark Zuckerberg, and Simon Sinek, knowing that their collective contributions have immeasurable business implications. Family and friends also play an important role in the would-be entrepreneur's quest for knowledge. Thus, it is evident aspiring business professionals understand the undeniable power of intelligence and how it alone shapes a company and their decisions. However, being well versed about the inner workings of business strategy and theory is only a fraction of what it will take to develop a successful business enterprise.

For individuals who are a novice to the business field and seek knowledge from trusted sources, it is important not to become frustrated as those sources are often heavily inundated with business jargon. If individuals are not careful, their inquiry can have an adverse effect on pursuing an entrepreneurial endeavor. Therefore, this book aims to simplify the process without sacrificing critical content. For starters, it covers seven key topics which will help readers who are seriously considering unleashing their entrepreneurial aspirations.

Step one is to "See It," which focuses on the importance of having a vision and mission that guides the work you do.

The second step is to "Seize It," which focuses on developing a strong business plan that adheres to the mission, vision, and governance of your prospective company. Step three is to "Scrutinize It," as no successful business has reached the pinnacle of success without seeking feedback, consultation, knowledge gathering, conducting a SWOT analysis (a study undertaken by an organization to identify its internal strengths and weaknesses, as well as its external opportunities and threats), and gaining an understanding of consumer behavior. Step four is to "Simplify It," and not in a mediocre or remedial sense but simply answering the "why" of your business. The fifth step is to "Sell It," and not in a literal sense as it relates to acquisition but how you plan to sell/pitch your products or services to your prospective stakeholders. The sixth step is to "Sustain It," as most business ventures fail because no one truly considered planning for growth and sustainability.

Lastly, but most importantly, step seven is to "Support It," as many businesses collapse because the owner or owners fail to assemble a team which can carry out its mission and vision at all levels of the organization. Let us begin to "See It" beyond our imagination to a more narrowed approach to ensure our vision is not steeped in misguided passion, but is responding precisely to satisfying a need in which consumers and customers alike are willing to support.

If you are working on something exciting that you really care about, you don't have to be pushed. The vision pulls you.

—*Steve Jobs*

Chapter One
See It

IRECALL READING A STORY ABOUT OPRAH WINFREY FEATURED on her website which reflected on her childhood. It stated that when she was a young girl, she watched her grandmother hang clothes and vividly remembers her grandmother stating, "Oprah Gail, you better watch me now, 'cause one day you gon' have to know how to do this for yourself."

In 1954 when Oprah was born until this defining moment in her life, I imagine she never thought she would top the Forbes List in 2013 for being the most powerful celebrity. Her accomplishments are vast but her vision, in my opinion, far surpasses any financial or humanitarian achievement she will ever accomplish. In fact, history is clear. Mississippi in the 1950s was perhaps one of the worst places for an African American child to be born and for most children of color, Oprah's grandmother's advice was spot on.

How does this vivid memory of Oprah's childhood relate to the vision of an aspiring entrepreneur? Successful entrepreneurs can have varied paths toward success but whether they began their business empire in a garage, dorm room, or on a park bench, it all began with a vision. A vision which most people cannot see and if would-be entrepreneurs sought validation from others, they would likely receive harsh criticisms because their vision exceeds the vision of their critics. Similar to Oprah, perhaps you do not know what your next big business venture will be, but like Oprah are you confident in knowing what you will not become in the face of those who attempt to limit your options. The question, I believe should never be avoided or even slightly dismissed is, "Do you see it for yourself?" Perhaps you are in the beginning stages of developing your business idea but you have unfortunately allowed others to steal both your vision and motivation to move your idea into a tangible business solution.

The biggest casualty of poor vision is that it robs you of your most valuable asset, which is time. Business mogul and investor Mark Cuban once said, "Time is the most valuable asset you don't own. You may or may not realize it yet, but how you use or don't use your time is going to be the best indication of where your future is going to take you." Businesses fail for a myriad of reasons, but having a poor or undefined vision will surely destroy any hope of becoming a successful business owner. It is imperative you do not waste your time trying to convince others to see what you see. The truth is, it's your vision birthed out of your own instincts and response to what you believe is possible, not what naysayers would contend. Many of the great inventors defied popular opinion and chased their vision with or without the support of the masses. Jobs, Gates, Edison, the Wright brothers, Ford, and countless others did not waste time trying to get others to see their vision, but silenced and astounded their critics by doing what hadn't been done in history.

Once you have overcome the hurdle of not being consumed with the opinions of others, you can focus on the next challenge of your vision which is seizing the opportunities that allow your vision to move from a concept to a feasible business plan. The ability to support your vision with opportunities that you can seize will be a critical step in developing your business plan. The savviest entrepreneur takes pride in figuring out the process to eliminate any potential threats to their business and attempts to mitigate any known obstacles. However, it is wise to balance having a critical lens with being capable of ensuring your vision comes to fruition. Sadly, many great business ventures fail in the vision phase primarily because the vision itself becomes stagnate and compromised.

Sometimes in this life, only one or two opportunities are put before us, and we must seize them, no matter the risk.

—Andre Dubus III

Chapter Two
Seize It

THE VISION YOU HAVE CREATED FOR YOUR POTENTIAL business is crystal clear. To others, it might be confusing because they cannot be as confident about your endeavor as you are. Since it's not their vision, they cannot see the merit in it. Therefore, the key is to ensure your vision is well defined and has some fluidity. Successful entrepreneurs are prone to make mistakes, but they welcome constructive feedback to perfect their overall vision. Doing so puts them in a better position to seize opportunities that support their efforts.

The first and best lesson entrepreneurs must learn is that all opportunities are not worth exploring. Some so-called opportunities are not really opportunities at all but are underdeveloped ideas that can waste time and drain limited resources. In the beginning phases of your business venture, you will have a seemingly insatiable hunger to pursue any and all opportunities you perceive will advance your vision. Much needed traits such as optimism and intuition that many successful business people possess are useful but these can also betray you and lead to disillusionment and eventually the collapse of your business. Therefore, performing a cost-benefit analysis will allow you to make sound financial judgments.

In short, a cost-benefit analysis is a strategic approach used to determine the cost of moving forward with an opportunity based upon the potential benefits. Thus, it is im-

perative to strategically explore achievable opportunities uti-
lizing strategy as an evaluation tool. For example, you have
spent years working as an automobile mechanic and have
earned a decent living doing so. Now the desire to run your
own shop is urging you to take that entrepreneurial leap. For
the past ten years, you have worked on weekends outside of
your garage and consequently; you have built a large customer base. One day you are approached by one of your
customers asking if you would be interested in purchasing an
old abandoned shop about 15 miles away from your home.
Initially, you dismissed the opportunity. You feel that you
have done well for yourself over the years as a part-time mechanic. Abandoning your job to start a full-time business at
this point in life could be too risky. However, your inquisitive-
ness and passion for auto mechanics had you waking up an
hour early to drive by the location and instantly you felt the
opportunity was worth exploring. The question is, is inquis-
itiveness and passion enough to engage the inherent risks of
entrepreneurship?

This scenario is a frequent opportunity for most would-be
entrepreneurs because I contend when you develop a vision,
it inherently attracts opportunities. The difference between
successful and unsuccessful opportunities are how they are
approached. It would not be an accurate assumption to suggest that all failed businesses were destined to fail. However,
I believe many businesses could have obtained success if the
business owners were more strategic in their decisions. In the
stated example, it might be wise to find out how a new automobile shop will thrive in that area and what happened to
the previous business. Perhaps the previous business had too
many competitors or could not compete with the on-site service centers within major car dealerships.

Before mortgaging the house and securing the financial resources needed to purchase the shop, a cost-benefit analysis will provide some key insights as to whether the purchase would be a great investment and business venture. Given the benefits far outweigh the cost, the decision is clear that acquiring the shop aligns with the mechanic's vision of ownership, coupled with his ability to provide a service that is in high demand. However, before you begin to purchase a new property, it is best to take a step back and develop a sound business plan.

When it comes to developing a business plan, like most things, there are varying viewpoints. However, I believe entrepreneur and Forbes Magazine contributor Patrick Hull has a sound approach to developing a strong and effective business plan using ten key components. He uses the following components when he is considering an investment:

1. Mission statement and/or vision statement so you articulate what you're trying to create;

2. Description of your company and product or service;

3. Description of how your product or service is different;

4. Market analysis that discusses the market you're trying to enter, competitors, where you fit, and what type of market share you believe you can secure;

5. Description of your management team, including the experience of key team members and previous successes;

6. How you plan to market the product or service;

7. Analysis of your company's strengths, weaknesses,

opportunities, and threat, which will show that you're realistic and have considered opportunities and challenges;

8. Develop a cash flow statement so you understand what your needs are now and will be in the future (a cash flow statement also can help you consider how cash flow could impact growth);

9. Revenue projections; and

10. Summary/conclusion that wraps everything together (this also could be an executive summary at the beginning of the plan).

In my opinion, the components of Hull's approach are extremely useful and have proven to be effective. One thing that entrepreneurs quickly learn is you do not have to reinvent the wheel at every turn. Many successful business owners and advisors have left paths that can be followed. Instead of claiming to offer a new framework for success, it is better to offer you an approach that works. There is no shame in offering the wisdom of someone who's achieved success. I firmly believe many businesses fail in the infancy stages of their development because they do not understand how important a strong business plan is correlated to their overall success. Hull's plan is thorough as there are many examples that attempt to offer alluring suggestions for a business plan, but they lack depth and true functionally for the novice entrepreneur.

As stated in the opening chapter, a vision and/or mission statement is essential to forming a business. Additionally, being able to effectively describe your company's products or services is critical, but it is equally important if you desire ultimate success to offer some level of differentiation to attract customers in the market. As you move throughout the business plan, be intentional and strategic to ensure your business plan clearly articulates your goals because you always should be prepared to pitch your business plan to a prospective investor. To be clear, you do not have to be obligated to any particular business plan template, but regardless of which plan you use, be certain it is polished and professional. At this stage in your business development, it's essential that you have a clear vision of your business and you are strategically prepared to seize opportunities as they arise. While you are waiting to seize the next opportunity, scrutinize and tweak your plan to maximize your strength while minimizing your weaknesses.

ness is successful. Performing a SWOT analysis is a useful tool when assessing if your product or service is a good fit for the market as it focuses on your strengths, weaknesses, opportunities, and threats. These actions, while perhaps appearing cumbersome, will allow you to scrutinize your business and make refinements where necessary to improve your overall outcomes. Once you have completed this process, your work does not stop there but instead, you need to simplify your vision to answer "the why" of your business.

When you're first thinking through an idea, it's important not to get bogged down in complexity. Thinking simply and clearly, is hard to do.
—*Paul Branson*

Chapter Four
Simplify It

CONSUMER BEHAVIOR IS THE PRIMARY FOCUS OF MARKETING psychologists who study and analyze the buying habits of consumers which informs the development of marketing strategy and campaigns. However, most times the entrepreneur has to take on this role and attempt to understand the ebb and flow of their potential customers and clients. To say the least, this can be a daunting task. However, I do not think an Ivy League education makes one more or less capable of understanding their customers. To be clear, this is not a slight at traditional forms of education, but I have seen business owners achieve great levels of success without having any formal education. For example, John a local restaurant owner in New York has been in business for forty years and despite the fluctuations in the restaurant industry, he has remained a vibrant staple in the business community. Technology innovation icon Steve Jobs found formal schooling boring and would later leave college to pursue his interest in electronics. He and his business partner Steve Wozniak literally built their business in a garage and would later amass unparalleled success.

When I started my lemonade stand, I did not know about the financial terminology of credits and debits but in a general sense, I understood I needed to make more money than my mother spent to buy the ingredients and the supplies. For those who have the privilege to attend the Gies College of Business, I am certain your efforts and business prowess will afford you great outcomes. For those like Jobs who find school less alluring, I encourage you not to abandon your entrepreneurial endeavor. You will probably have to work harder and continually learn to ensure your success. Honestly, it does not matter if we are talking about a Harvard alum or a college dropout from the Bronx, both would-be entrepreneurs need to answer the question of why their product or service adds value to the consumer and meets their needs.

While in the MBA program, we studied several different Harvard business cases, but one case I found extremely interesting was the introduction of the Segway HT, the two-wheeled self-balancing personal transporter that you often see in airports and shopping malls. While Segway is still produced today, the initial market launch grossly fell below expectations. While I am not attempting to analyze the marketing strategy of Segway or their business plan, I do vividly remember when they appeared on Good Morning America in 2001. I was shocked at the price, the design, and the overall concept. I was asking myself "who would want this mode of transportation?"

Unsurprisingly, Segway did not capture the market segment they had hoped for but was able to sell their product to police departments, airports, warehouses, and other similar entities. Whether we are talking about Segway or the entrepreneur who wants to start a new business building the best widget, you must answer this question, "why would consumers choose your product or service?" Had Segway analyzed the heart of this question, past their product zeal, they may have changed their marketing and launch plans and saved themselves a lot of money and embarrassment. Entrepreneurs cannot fail to ask and answer this crucial question.

If I am an executive in a downtown suite, why am I turning in my Mercedes Benz keys to commute to work on a Segway? If I am a connoisseur of food, why am I paying a premium price and traveling 20 miles to dine in a particular restaurant? When you are developing your business, you are most often excited and believe everyone will be equally enthused, but failure to discover why someone should choose your product or service over someone else's could cost you big-time. Once you have effectively answered the question of why, you can then begin to sell your business to prospective consumers and your stakeholders.

I have never worked a day in my life without selling. If I believe in something, I sell it, and I sell it hard.

—*Estee Lauder*

Chapter Five
Sell It

THE HIT TELEVISION SHOW SHARK TANK HAS RESONATED with millions of viewers and would-be entrepreneurs who believe that they could have the next successful business or product. However, before you show up to the next Shark Tank casting call, you would be wise to consider that the show only deals with one critical aspect of a business and that is securing investors. Of course, the competing entrepreneurs are showcasing their products and services using their best pitch, but the Sharks are not easily swayed. Asking questions about past, current, and projected sales is a key inquiry expressed by the Sharks as they want to determine whether the entrepreneur's valuation is overzealous or conservative. Nonetheless, selling or pitching your business idea to a venture capitalist is not the only selling you will do in order to have a successful business. In fact, you will have to sell to your board of directors, employees, suppliers, local community, elected government officials, and customers, just to name a few key players.

I can imagine Steve Jobs and Tesla CEO, Elon Musk have had tough conversations with the board of directors as their innovative genius is likely not always celebrated, but deemed as a costly liability to the company. In some cases, the tensions are so high that the entrepreneur exits the company or takes on a different role or even starts a new business venture. For example, Jobs left his position at Apple amid some internal conflict. Harland Sanders expressed great disappointment toward some of his business partners as he felt they had abandoned his vision for KFC. Without implying conjecture or speculation, I am certain Musk will have some fallout with his board members. Regardless of these inherent tensions, the entrepreneur must effectively engage at all levels of the organization.

Employees are a huge factor in a company's success. It is not happenstance that Walmart has huge meetings to get their managers excited about their responsibility to ensure they perform with a high level of accountability. Establishing a great relationship with suppliers is also important for a restaurant owner, just as it is for a cellular telephone company trying to secure internal microchips for their new product launch.

As an entrepreneur, if you fail to establish a good working relationship with the local community and government officials, you will likely run into avoidable obstacles. Imagine that your business is growing faster than expected and expansion is inevitable, but you are at odds with the local community and elected officials which issue the permits and signatures you would need to obtain approval for expansion.

It is important to understand that having great relationships with the local community and elected officials should never be at the expense of not operating with the highest level of ethical standards. Lastly, but certainly not least, you continually have to sell and satisfy your customers to build brand loyalty and maintain their trust. These relationships are fluid, and adjustments must continuously be made to ensure they remain strong and intact.

When you have achieved success like Apple, Oprah, Nike, or even the small convenience store, you must be committed to sustaining it. Success is not guaranteed as there are many companies, despite their longevity, that have folded like Circuit City, Carson's, Woolworth, Nokia, and many more. Thus, success is measured not just in the now, but for its sustainability.

I'm here to build something for long-term. Anything else is a distraction.

—*Mark Zuckerberg*

Chapter Six

Sustain It

THE EXCITEMENT IS OVERWHELMING WHEN YOU FIRST form your business, despite all the barriers you have to overcome. Regardless of the adversities you encounter, you must plan strategically for great success. For example, when you were selling cakes and pies to family members during the holiday season, you did not realize that you were filling more than 200 orders. You didn't mind it then, because you were equipped to handle that. However, after you started selling pastries to the public, you were averaging 200-plus orders in a week. The increase was great, but along with it came all the stress of meeting increasing demand. You quickly made adjustments in your schedule and even streamlined your prepping process to keep up with demand, but you failed to think long-term such as, hiring more staff and leasing commercial kitchen space, as your business grew. Therefore, you could not meet the demand of your consumers which consequently caused your business to suffer.

In retrospect, you realized you never had a solid plan for growth. You never really quantified the sure amount of time and effort it would take to sustain success. I believe Mark Cuban provides a chilling reality for entrepreneurs stating, "Work like there is someone working 24 hours a day to take it all away from you." The reality is if you fail to meet customer expectations, they will likely abandon your product or service and find a suitable alternative. Ultimate business success is not having a powerful opening or launch and a few years of meeting or exceeding expectations, but it is reflected in your grit and the ability to achieve long-term sustainability.

Joel Osteen pastors a church in Houston, Texas where he became the senior pastor upon the death of his father John Osteen. Lakewood Church has a 16,800 seat capacity as it was the former Compaq Center where the National Basketball Association (NBA) team, the Houston Rockets, played their home games. I imagine at the time of the purchase of the facility the congregation could not fill the worship center but clearly, the Osteen family expected massive growth where such a facility would be a necessity. I am not sure if Warren Buffet, the original owner of the property, community members, or even the congregants understood the business decision behind purchasing the massive property. Nonetheless, Lakewood Church had a long-term strategy for growth and sustainability which has proven to be successful. They now average more than 50,000 visitors per week and have no signs of slowing down. Whether we are talking about a megachurch, Johnson & Johnson, Tyler Perry Studios, a local bakery, or a major automobile manufacturer, it is imperative to plan for growth as failure to do so will cause any entrepreneur to encounter avoidable setbacks.

For many entrepreneurs, such an oversight can cause irreversible damage. Therefore, purchasing a bakery shop that has the capacity to produce 2,000-5,000 baked goods per week gives the entrepreneur the needed flexibility for growth. It is truly unwise to not account for growth and sustainability because if you achieve success, you can be assured would-be competitors will fearlessly come after your product or service. Growth and sustainability are not only wedded to production, but must be applied broadly throughout the organization. For example, how will your organization attract and retain its employees or how will you market your product or service and what will be your strategies to attract multiple consumer segments? These questions should always be at the forefront of the entrepreneur's thought process and included in all efforts made toward sustainability.

At this phase in your process, you have achieved success but the last and final step is just as critical as the preceding ones because success is rarely achieved in isolation. Assembling a productive and effective team is just as important as the creative genius of the founders. Understanding how to lead, motivate, and support the efforts of your team will prove to be one of the most important roles as an entrepreneur. It is invigorating to be a part of something that is great and given that you are adequately supported, the work feels more meaningful despite the inherent demands for excellence.

Coming together is the beginning, staying together is progress, and working together is success.

—Henry Ford

Chapter Seven

Support It

AT EVERY LEVEL OF YOUR ORGANIZATION, YOU HAVE TO BE assured your employees are adhering to the mission and vision of the company. This is best accomplished when employees feel a part of the team where their voices matter and they are confident their work adds significant value. Company culture is difficult to change; therefore entrepreneurs should be mindful of what types of policies and procedures they wish to implement to support the culture they desire to establish. Each year companies like Bain & Company, Johnson & Johnson, Google, Facebook, and Southwest Airlines are ranked among the top companies for the best places to work.

The similarity of these diverse organizations is their ability to create an atmosphere that demands excellence but ensures their employees are well supported in the process. At the Chief Executive Officer (CEO) level the primary goal is to yield the greatest profit for the shareholders which for some entrepreneurs translates to having lean salaries and employee benefits. For some employees, their primary goal is to obtain the maximum earning potential for their assigned job, but this seems to be in direct conflict to the CEO who desires to maximize profits.

Therefore, successful entrepreneurs find a way to strike a healthy balance. Companies like Southwest Airlines provide their employees with profit sharing opportunities which demonstrates the company's commitment to their hourly workers, not just to their high ranking executives. Facebook offers several alluring benefits to their employees like four months of paid time off for new parents within the first year of birth or adoption, student loan payoffs, a fitness center, and even an on-site health and dental care facility are among a few of the perks offered to their employees. Why would a company spend such an absorbent amount of money on employee benefits given the high turnover rates among millennials? The answer is simple, extremely successful companies like Facebook and Google understand the fiercely competitive environment for talent and want to ensure their employees are beyond satisfied because their satisfaction has a direct correlation to the company's overall success.

For the new entrepreneurs, I am not suggesting you build an on-site cleaners for your employees, but you must be mindful of how you are supporting your employees because they are on the front lines of ensuring your mission and vision are accomplished. An organization large or small will be equipped with a janitor and a CEO but how do we make sure they both appreciate their respective roles. This is the finesse and savviness of a successful entrepreneur because they are committed to providing all of their employees irrespective of their pay and position, a level of appreciation that shows just how much they value their service to the company.

Having your employees feel a high sense of satisfaction is a key component of supporting your organization and failure to do so will cause employees to stay and produce subpar results, or leave the company in search of an organization that adheres to their needs of being valued and supported by their employer. Although this seems to be an obvious strategy for the would-be entrepreneur, it is often an overlooked step and causes many businesses to fail in the early years of their organization.

Entrepreneurship is living a few years of your life like most people won't, so that you can spend the rest of your life like most people can't.

—Unknown

Success is relative, but for those who desire to achieve greatness as an entrepreneur it means they are committed to working unbelievably hard to ensure their dreams come true and once they do, they commit to working even harder to sustain it.

—Eugene L. Moore, MBA, Ph.D.

Conclusion

S TARTING A BUSINESS CAN BE STRESSFUL BUT IF YOU CAN BE strategic in your approach, you can minimize some of the inherent pressures business ownership entails. The purpose of this book is to encourage an aspiring entrepreneur to chase their dreams with intentionality by applying strategic decisions across their entire business concept. The first stage of figuring out if your business idea has merit is to move it from the internal workings of your brain to a tangible reality. This is why it is imperative for the entrepreneur to *See It*, which is best achieved when they develop a mission statement and vision. The anxieties that exist when establishing a business are real and consequently, your hunger for success can cloud your judgment. Therefore, it is undeniably imperative to understand how to pursue strategic opportunities because if you fail to *Seize It*, your opportunity cost will be greater than you can afford.

The ability to *Scrutinize It* is important but first starts with figuratively developing skin like Teflon because failure and rejection are unavoidable. It is important to anticipate failure and rejection and allow them to be fueled into lessons that can ignite success. Once this skill is developed, you can honestly seek feedback and interrogate your business plan for weaknesses and opportunities for improvement. As a writer, motivational speaker, and researcher, I am prone to over explain but as an entrepreneur, it is necessary to *Simplify It*, so that prospective stakeholders can clearly articulate "the why" of your business. Understanding "the why" of your business makes the *Sell It* step so much easier as people are less inclined to question your product or service because they are assured it meets their current and future needs. It seems that if you have successfully completed the first five steps, the entrepreneur can be safely unleashed but the last two steps are just as critical and detrimental if not correctly applied. Understanding how to *Sustain It* and *Support It* is imperative.

I imagine Jobs and Zuckerberg anticipated the measures they would have to take to sustain and support their business enterprise. A great business plan, a creative marketing strategy, and an impressive valuation might be sufficient to woo prospective investors, but the greatest investment any company can make is in its people. Creating a company culture that attracts and retains superior talent is essential for your success and sustainability. Although cliché, great companies are comprised of great people, developing support mechanisms for your employees is important. Preparing for growth across the entire organization will perhaps lead to global prominence or local dominance, either way, your goal should always be to support the people who allow your vision to materialize.

As you begin to read the final words of this book, I encourage you to not give up on your business venture. Whether you are an educated alum of a prestigious university or a blue-collar worker with a dream to own a business, it is my hope this book helped you to discover, *The Business in You, Unleashing the Entrepreneur* starts with your vision and ends with your ability to invite others to be a part of a shared vision. You are equipped with the ability to build and sustain a great organization that withstands the punches entrepreneurship inherently invites. Welcome to the world of business ownership where you can boldly endorse the front of your check knowing that you have the power to shape the lives of so many because of your unwavering ability to turn your vision into a viable business.

About the Publisher

Let us bring your story to life! Life to Legacy offers the following publishing services: manuscript development, editing, transcription services, ghostwriting, cover design, copyright services, ISBN assignment, worldwide distribution, and eBooks.

Throughout the entire production process, you maintain control over your project. Even if you have no manuscript, we can ghostwrite your story for you from audio recordings or legible handwritten documents. Whether print-on-demand or trade publishing, we have publishing packages to meet your needs. We make the production and publishing processes easy for you.

We also specialize in family history books so that you can leave a written legacy for your children, grandchildren, and others. You put your story in our hands, and we'll bring it to literary life!

Please visit our website:
www.Life2Legacy.com
Or call us at:
877-267-7477
You can also e-mail us at:
Life2Legacybooks@att.net

CPSIA information can be obtained
at www.ICGtesting.com
Printed in the USA
LVHW011607190122
708805LV00011B/86